The Power of the Class 31s

Plate 1: In original green livery with contrasting bands, but with a yellow warning panel added to the front, between the bands, Type 2 A1A-A1A No. D5835 emerges from Copenhagen Tunnel, on the climb up Holloway Bank towards Finsbury Park, on 17th May 1961. The train for Grantham consists of mainly maroon stock, with a Gresley buffet car as the fourth vehicle. Two years after the photograph was taken, this locomotive was fitted with an uprated Mirrlees engine that developed 2,000b.h.p. and acquitted itself well on several Type 4 and Type 5 timings, including some 'Deltic' turns.

Brian Morrison

Plate 2: Passing beneath the North London line at Belle Isle, between Gasworks and Copenhagen tunnels, No. 5610 lifts a long rake of empty coaching stock away from King's Cross, and up the bank towards Hornsey Carriage Sidings on a sunny 22nd March 1973.

Brian Morrison

The Power of the Class 31s

Brian Morrison

Oxford Publishing Company

Copyright © 1984 Brian Morrison &
Oxford Publishing Co.

ISBN 0-86093-064-5

All rights reserved. No part of this book may be reproduced or transmitted in any form or by any means, electronic or mechanical, including photocopying, recording or any information storage and retrieval system, without permission in writing from the Publisher.

Typesetting by:
Aquarius Typesetting Services, New Milton, Hants.

Printed in Great Britain by:
Biddles Ltd, Guildford, Surrey.

Published by:
Oxford Publishing Co.
Link House
West Street
POOLE, Dorset

Plate 3: An attractive scene near Portcreek Junction, on 12th June 1982. Crossing the Broom Channel, just north of Hilsea, No. 31165 heads the 16.10 Portsmouth Harbour to Cardiff (Central) service away from Portsea Island, and passes Class 416/3(4CAP) electric multiple unit No. 3302, which forms the 15.16 Brighton to Portsmouth harbour 'Coastway' service. Travelling via Southampton, Salisbury and Bristol (Temple Meads), the five Mk. I bogies make for easy timing, with the Class 31/1 due to arrive in the Welsh capital at 19.42.

Brian Morrison

Introduction

The British Transport Commission's 1955 modernisation plan, incorporating its now notorious 'pilot scheme' for diesel locomotive construction, provided for an assortment of different designs to be built, in small batches, to allow for comparative testing. As it transpired, this edict allowed much wider scope for private builders than was prudent and the result was a large number of differing locomotive types of many shapes and sizes, ranging from the good to the downright appalling. As a result, the decade to follow found British Railways in somewhat of a state of flux but, from the unhappy state of affairs, some well-designed and efficient locomotives did emerge. One of these was the Type 2 design of A1A-A1A wheel arrangement, constructed at the Loughborough Works of Brush Engineering and later becoming known as the Class 31. Powered by their subsidiary company's Mirrlees V12 cylinder, turbocharged, four stroke, 1,250b.h.p engine, the JVS12T, the first of the type, was delivered for trials in October 1957. It then commenced revenue-earning service the following month while allocated to Stratford Depot in East London, numbered D5500.

The first batch of twenty locomotives appeared at the rate of approximately two per month, and their success was such that subsequent orders were soon placed. Over the ensuing years their non-standard electromagnetic engine control system was replaced with the more conventional electro-pneumatic type, the disc headcode system was changed to roller blind route indicator panels and their engines were uprated to 1,365b.h.p. to provide more punch. Their arena of operation stretched from the original East Anglian workings from Liverpool Street, to Devon, South Wales, the Midlands, Yorkshire and the North-East, plus services from King's Cross and Paddington, with occasional sorties into Southern Region territory. However, operation rarely extended into Cornwall, or north of Edinburgh, in Scotland.

From 1964, the engines were replaced on all 263 members of the class, by English Electric 12SVTs, rated at 1,470b.h.p. The original green livery with two contrasting bands was also changed to standard British Rail blue, the roller blinds were taken out and replaced with marker lights, and the classifications became 31/0 for the original batch of twenty electromagnetic locomotives, 31/1 for the standard types, and 31/4 for those modified for dual or electric train heating. All the changes that have occurred, the variety of duties to which they have been rostered over the years, and the geographical area that they cover have been included in this album, which covers the life and times of the Class 31s from the mid-1950s to the present day.

Brian Morrison
Sidcup, Kent.
April 1984

Plate 4: On 5th September 1980, No. 31129 enters Horbury Cutting, near Healey Mills, while hauling an eastbound freight that appears to consist of, amongst other things, chemical tanks, a four wheel van, a coal hopper, a string of bogie bolsters and some 'Presflo' wagons; a load that can safely be described as a mixed one! The locomotive is one of those constructed without route indicator panels, due to a problem with their supply at the time.

Brian Morrison

THE 'TOFFEE APPLES'

Plate 5: The original twenty locomotives of the class, later classified as 31/0, acquired the nickname of 'Toffee Apples' due to the shape of the removable power handles, as illustrated below In this view of the assembly line at the Loughborough Works of Brush Traction, the first six members of the class are near completion and will soon be numbered D5500−5.

Colin J. Marsden Collection

Plate 6: Class 31/0 cab layout
1. Power controller and master switch (known as the 'Toffee Apple').
2. Locomotive brake controller.
3. Train brake controller.
4. Brake cylinder pressure gauge.
5. Vacuum chamber/train pipe gauge.
6. Main generator ammeter.
7. Speed indicator.
8. Engine start button.
9. Engine stopped indicator button.
10. Engine stopped indicator light.
11. Wheel slip indicator light.
12. General alarm indicator light.

Colin J. Marsden

Plate 7: The first main line diesel-electric locomotive to be delivered to the Eastern Region, is seen on its first booked passenger train working. Here No. D5500 makes the scheduled stop at Thorpe-le-Soken, on 13th November 1957, in charge of the 10.36 Liverpool Street to Clacton service.

Frank Greygoose

Plate 8: The same train arrives at its Clacton destination, with the driver and a number of passengers and onlookers making a variety of faces for the official photograph of the occasion.

Frank Greygoose

Plate 9: In original condition of dark green livery, grey roof and pale green stripes and window surrounds, No. D5506 crosses Barking Flyover and approaches Barking Station, on 25th March 1959, with a very mixed freight.
Colin J. Marsden Collection

Plate 10: All the class are mounted on an interesting wheel layout known as A1A-A1A which employs the curious use of smaller wheels on the unpowered centre axle of each bogie, no attempt having been made to slim down the design to a more conventional Bo-Bo arrangement. The resultant locomotive of over 100 tons was to be criticised for a poor power to weight ratio but, in truth, a number of years passed before a diesel-electric type appeared with more power for less weight. Here No. D5505 passes Brentwood & Warley Station, in September 1957, hauling a heavy ten coach Norwich express on the climb up Brentwood Bank towards Ingrave Summit.
Stanley Creer

Plate 11 (right): Another view photographed at the same location as that in *Plate 10*, but looking in the opposite direction. On 14th June 1958, No. D5509 races down Brentwood Bank with a Liverpool Street-bound express from Norwich.
Stanley Creer

Plate 12 (below): A special train load of Hartmann Fibre Company's containers, photographed just outside Great Yarmouth on 10th December 1959, is headed by No. D5500. On the original batch of twenty locomotives the jumper cables were fitted to the opposite side of the coupling hook, in order to avoid coupling confusion between electromagnetic and electro-pneumatic types.
Frank Greygoose

Plate 13: A Class B1 4-6-0 locomotive slogs up the bank towards Ingrave Summit, in September 1957, while hauling a rake of four-wheeled vans, and contrasts with Type 2 No. D5511, which is heading towards the capital with an express from Norwich. This was the locomotive which was sent to the Scottish Region for trials in July 1958, one of the rare occasions when an example of the class strayed north of Edinburgh.

Stanley Creer

Plate 14: On a sunny May day, in 1959, No. D5512 runs into Liverpool Street with empty stock. The headboard for 'The Essex Coast Express', propped up on the platform in front of the Class B1 4-6-0, probably means that the stock will form the well-known 17.27 service to Clacton, headed by a 'Britannia' class Pacific.

Martin Welch

Plate 15 (left): With traction cables emerging from the engine-room, No. D5506 is pictured inside the Doncaster Works Test House in May 1965.
Colin J. Marsden Collection

Plate 16: An immaculate No. D5518, with a half yellow front warning panel, prepares to depart from Dagenham Dock Yard, on 4th May 1964, with a load of Mk. I Ford Cortinas and Ford Zodiacs bound for Bathgate in Scotland. This locomotive was the only one of the original twenty to be fitted with electro-pneumatic coupling and headcode boxes, following accident repair at Doncaster Works, when only standard ends were available as replacements.
Frank Greygoose

Plate 17: For a short time, the original numbers allocated to the class were retained, even though the livery had been changed to standard British Rail blue with full yellow front. Posing at Stratford, on 10th August 1973, No. 5514 has been shorn of the 'D' number prefix but still retains the bodyside footsteps beside the cab door, which gave access to the roof hatch for water replenishment. Throughout the entire class they were fitted from new, but have since been sheeted over.

Brian Morrison

Plate 18: On ex-London, Tilbury & Southend Railway metals No. 5507 approaches Purfleet, on 7th March 1973, with a trip working from Ripple Lane, Barking.

Brian Morrison

Plate 19 (above): Now with its new T.O.P.S. number of 31012, the thirteenth member of the class passes Streatham Hill, in third rail territory, with a Stratford to East Croydon parcels train, on 27th July 1974.

Stanley Creer

Plate 20 (below): A work-stained No. 31002 threads a path through Stratford on 28th September 1979 while hauling a rake of oil tanks.

John G. Glover

Plate 21 (right): Retaining the silver roof provided by Stratford for the RPPR special of 22nd October 1977, illustrated in *Plate 26*, No. 31019 receives a clean under the Stratford Diesel Depot's washer unit, on a sunny 6th February 1979.
Colin J. Marsden

Plate 22 (below): An interesting combination captured at Shepreth Branch Junction, between Cambridge and Shelford, on 18th October 1978. No. 31015 hauls Class 56 No. 56037 and Class 31/1 No. 31258. The Class 56 (since named *Richard Trevithick*) has received running gear attention at Stratford and the Class 31/1 is proceeding to Doncaster for overhaul, as Doncaster is the only workshop in the BREL system which undertakes repairs to the Class 31 fleet.
John C. Baker

Plate 23: On the last remnant of the old Maldon branch, No. 31004 shunts a delivery of steel for a firm that are adjacent to the line at Witham in Essex. Beyond the coal wagon is all that remains of the branch, a private siding that extends for about one quarter of a mile only. This scene was recorded on 5th September 1980.

Michael J. Collins

Plate 24: No. 31002, in profile, at Colchester Yard on 11th May 1977.

Brian Morrison

Plate 25: Emerging from an unpleasant autumn fog, Nos. 31005 and 31019 stop at Manningtree, on 15th October 1977, with an enthusiasts' special from Liverpool Street bound for Sheffield.
Brian Morrison

Plate 26: Just one week later, Stratford worked some of their 'magic', and the same pair of locomotives now have silver roofs, red buffers and white wheel rims for the RPPR 'Toffee Apple Farewell' railtour from Paddington to branches in the Bristol area. This pleasant scene of No. 31019 leading No. 31005 shows the train beside the lovely Kennet & Avon Canal, near Bedwyn, on the approaches to Crofton on the Berks & Hants line. Shortly after the 'farewell' tour, traction plans were changed and the 'Toffee Apples' remained in service until the early 1980s.
Terry G. Flinders

Plate 27 (above): Four 'pilot scheme' Class 31/0s that were withdrawn were put into departmental stock as non self-propelled carriage pre-heating units. The first two were dealt with in the late 1970s, with No. 31014 receiving departmental number ADB 968015, shown here at the rear of Bounds Green Depot, North London, on 26th July 1979.

Brian Morrison

Plate 28 (below): No. 31013 was afforded much more resplendent treatment and is shown outside Stratford Works, after conversion, carrying number ADB 968013 and its original green livery, with body stripes, white roof and a half yellow front end. No. 31002 became ADB 968016 and No. 31006 carried the number ADB 968017.

Barry J. Nicolle

Plate 29: With the exception of the first member of the class (which has been preserved) and the four converted to mobile heating units, the remainder of the 'Toffee Apples' all succumbed to the cutter's torch. All that remained of Nos. 31003 and 31005 in Doncaster Works scrapyard, on 10th August 1980, were these rather sad cab ends.
Brian Morrison

Plate 30: More 'Toffee Apples' meet their end at Doncaster on the same day. Constructed in 1957 the Class 31/0s were active for some 23 years and, during that period of time, covered many thousands of miles on a myriad of duties.
Brian Morrison

MIRRLEES DAYS

Plate 31 (above): A block working of forty AFP Bird's Eye insulated containers is hauled by No. D5535 at Breydon curve, Great Yarmouth, on 20th July 1959. This particular locomotive was the first of the class to be given a top speed of 90m.p.h., following a change in gear ratio and the fitting of air-cooled pistons.

Colin J. Marsden Collection

Plate 32 (below): The 07.15 Class F freight from Whitemoor Yard passes between Newport and Elsenham, on the Cambridge line, on 15th September 1959. It is hauled by the first of the class to receive a route indicator panel and off-white body stripes, No. D5530.

Frank Greygoose

Plate 33: From No. D5520, the first in the second batch of the class, a number of notable changes took place from the original twenty 'pilot scheme' locomotives. The light blue windscreen surrounds were painted green, to match the remainder of the livery, the electromagnetic multiple unit control was changed to electro-pneumatic, which allowed the class to work in multiple with other classes, and the Mirrlees engines were uprated from 1,250 to 1,365b.h.p. Here No. D5586 takes the fast road through Hadley Wood Station, at the head of a semi-fast King's Cross to Hatfield working.

Derek Cross

Plate 34: A contingent of scouts are camped beneath the Ouse Viaduct, on 6th August 1961, as one of the class passes above with an excursion from Enfield to Brighton.

Stanley Creer

Plate 35: A very well-composed and thought-out picture of No. D5553 at speed near Bishop's Stortford, with a service from Liverpool Street. The young onlookers and the deliberately slow shutter speed of the camera combine to produce a result that is pictorial in every sense of the word.

Frank Greygoose

Plate 36: The Type 2 fleet of Brush A1A-A1A locomotives were, in many ways, mixed traffic equivalents of the Class B1 4-6-0s of the LNER, the 'Hall' class 4-6-0s of the GWR and the 'Black Fives' of the LMS, being capable of turning their hands to nearly any type of duty. Here a local service from King's Cross is hauled up Holloway Bank, on 23rd May 1961, by No. D5672.

Brian Morrison

Plate 37: Although it closed for passenger services in November 1952, the branch line from Wickham Market to Framlingham remained open for freight traffic. In this view, No. D5549 is pictured at the little terminus on a peaceful-looking June day in 1962.

Stanley Creer

Plate 38: A very mixed collection of carriage stock has been unearthed for this Sheffield to Blackpool excursion, seen here at Belfield, near Rochdale, on 16th June 1962, headed by Nos. D5810 and D5820, working in multiple.

Richard S. Greenwood

Plate 39 (above): Passing the remains of the old Holloway & Caledonian Road Station, which closed in 1915, two very different Type 2 diesel-electric locomotives climb towards Finsbury Park with empty stock workings. In this scene, British Rail Bo-Bo No. D5069 (later to become Class 24 under T.O.P.S.) appears to be losing ground to Brush A1A-A1A No. D5682.

Brian Morrison

Plate 40 (below): No. D5526 passes Norwich Thorpe Junction, on a March day in 1960, with a fitted freight from Yarmouth (Vauxhall). This particular location has changed very little in the years since this photograph was taken, and is still easily recognisable today.

John C. Baker

Plate 41 (above): Running alongside the River Waveney, No. D5555 approaches Haddiscoe, in September 1963, while heading a York to Lowestoft service. Although the locomotive is one of the second batch that received roof-mounted route indicators, there were some production difficulties, and some of those which were intended to have the fitment emerged from Loughborough in original condition, in this respect.
Stanley Creer

Plate 42 (left): With a correctly-fitted roof indicator, the code 2B72 signifies that No. D5643 has charge of a King's Cross to Hatfield local service.
John G. Glover

Plate 43 (right): Following a rugby cup final at Wembley Stadium No. D5692 returns to Wigan from Wembley Hill on 13th May 1961, and passes West Ruislip.
C.R.L. Coles

Plate 44: A notable event at the Loughborough Works of Brush Traction Ltd., in February 1960, as the 100th Type 2 locomotive is lowered on to its bogies.

Colin J. Marsden Collection

WARNING PANELS APPEAR

Plate 45: In order to make their presence more obvious to track maintenance staff and the like, all main line diesels on BR were required to have their front ends painted yellow, from the early 1960s. With the panel nicely situated between the body stripes, No. D5640 runs down from Finsbury Park towards King's Cross, with a fascinating conglomeration of stock, to make up the 'Queen of Scots' Pullman, in August 1962.

Brian Morrison

Plate 46: On 11th September 1963, No. D5563 propels a single wagon and brake van out of North Walsham (Norfolk) en route for Mundesley-on-Sea, with what was then the daily pick-up freight.

Stanley Creer

Plate 47 (right): Hauling just three maroon coaches is No. D5616, making up the 16.10 (SO) Manchester (Central) to Sheffield train on 26th April 1966.

Martin Welch

Plate 48: On 22nd January 1962, the Mirrlees 1,365b.h.p. engine coupled to the Brush generator is lifted out of the engine compartment of No. D5553, inside the diesel repair shop at Stratford. With the original 1,250b.h.p. setting being uprated to a new standard of 1,365b.h.p., larger main generators were necessary, and larger traction motors could now also be fitted.

Frank Greygoose

Plate 49 (left): Heading a return football excursion from Wembley Hill (since renamed Wembley Complex), the driver of No. D5852 awaits the 'right away' on 27th April 1963.

C.R.L. Coles

Plate 50 (right): Another attractive scene on the old Mundesley branch, with the daily pick-up freight in the charge of the usual Brush Type 2 making the return trip to Norwich.

Stanley Creer

Plate 51 (left): A vintage 1960s scene from Norwich. One of the class that missed out being provided with a route indicator panel, No. D5543, departs with an express for Liverpool Street, while two more of the same class can be seen in the background along with an English Electric Type 3 (later Class 37) locomotive. Others after No. D5530 without headcode boxes are Nos. D5535, D5539, D5543, D5547, D5548, D5551, D5552, D5555, D5556, D5559 and D5562.

Stanley Creer

Plate 52: The passenger branch to Hadleigh in Suffolk ran from Bentley, north of Manningtree, but closed for such services in February 1932. Its utilisation as a freight line, however, continued for many years, as witness this September 1964 scene at Hadleigh Terminus after arrival of a freight working from Ipswich, headed by No. D5594.
Stanley Creer

Plate 53: A summer excursion from Sheffield to Blackpool is rostered to No. D5826 and crosses Nott Wood Viaduct at Cornholme, on the Copy Pit line from Todmorden to Burnley, on 6th August 1962.
Richard S. Greenwood

ALL YELLOW ENDS

Plate 54: A dull, murky evening at King's Cross sees three Brush Type 2s preparing to take out commuter trains. On the left, No. D5625 retains the not unattractive half yellow warning panel, which is neatly fitted in between the front extensions of the body stripes. Nos. D5587 and D5591, however, depict the next stage in the changing livery of BR locomotives, with the front stripes painted over with yellow but, otherwise, still in original colours.

E. Sargieson

Plate 55: On a much brighter 9th August 1969, another example of the intermediate green livery, with all yellow front, is No. D5678, which has just run round its train at Woodhall Junction in Lincolnshire. The freight had just arrived from the Horncastle branch, which closed to passengers some five years earlier, and has since had all the lines lifted. Observe the splendid ex-Great Northern Railway somersault signals.

John Vaughan

Plate 56 (left): A Class 8 Fakenham (East) to Norwich freight is seen here on what used to be a part of the Wells-next-the-Sea branch, on the North Norfolk coast, this section of line being closed to passenger traffic in October 1964. About to cross one of the many gated crossings that once existed on the line north of East Dereham is green-liveried No. D5652, captured by the camera on 10th July 1969. This, in fact, was the first member of the class to receive air-brakes, in 1968.

John Vaughan

Plate 57 (below): No. D5576, with a Class 4 fitted freight from Whitemoor Yard to Parkeston Quay, passes Thurston, east of Bury St Edmunds, on a dull June afternoon in 1968. The crates in the first wagon contain kits of parts for export to construct Triumph Herald cars.

John C. Baker

Plate 58: On just a few examples of the class, an attempt was made to retain an acceptable cosmetic appearance to the all yellow front end, by retaining the all-round stripes, but eventually all were given the mandatory treatment. On August bank holiday Monday 1962, No. D5822 climbs from Portsmouth (Lancashire) to Copy Pit Summit with an excursion from the Sheffield area to Blackpool.

Richard S. Greenwood

Plate 59: Despite yellow paint being applied to the entire front end of No. D5676, the original white stripes are already beginning to show through again as the locomotive passes Thurston, in June 1967, with a midday special freight working from Whitemoor Yard to Ipswich and Parkeston Quay.

John C. Baker

SPECIFICATIONS

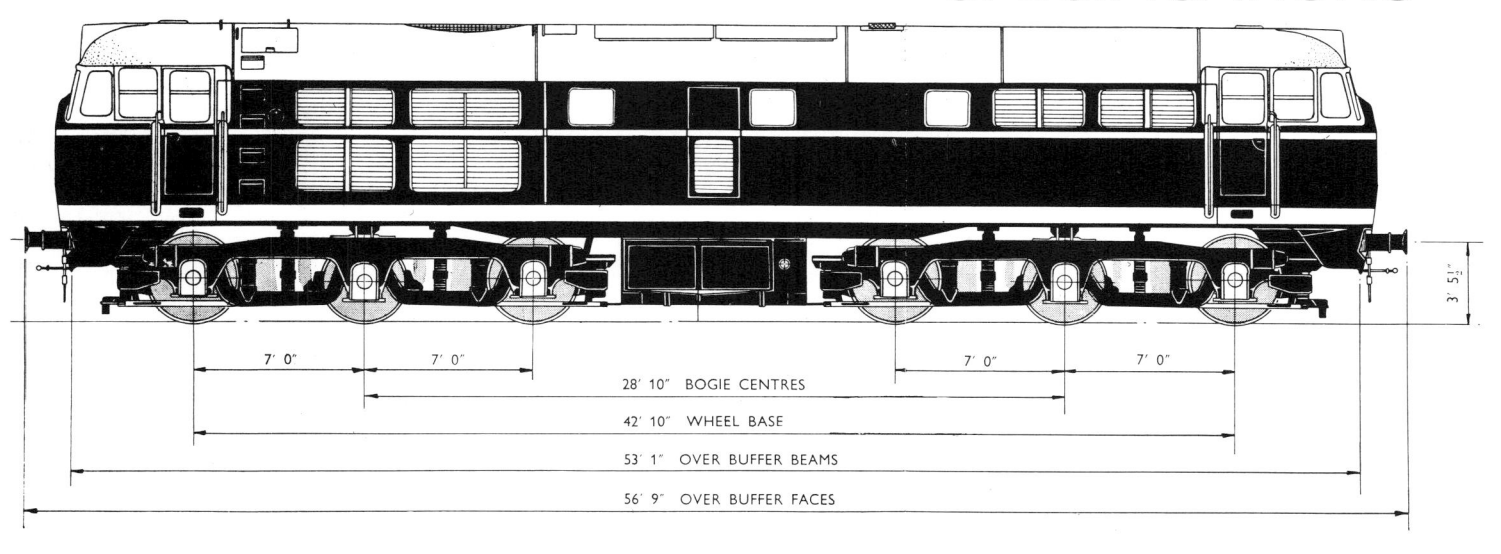

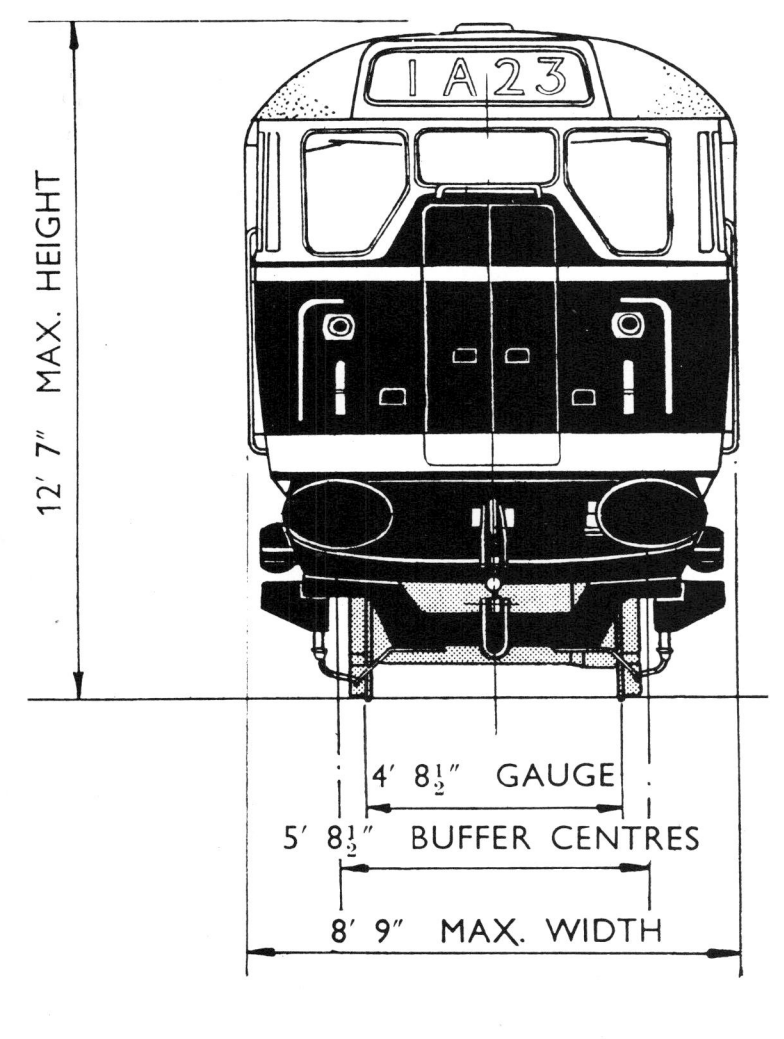

Overall length:	56ft.9in.
Overall height:	12ft.7in.
Overall width:	8ft.9in.
Overall wheelbase:	42ft.10in.
Driving wheel diameter:	3ft.7in.
Carrying wheel diameter:	3ft.3½in.
Locomotive weight as built:	104 tons
Locomotive weight as re-engined:	107 tons
Brake force:	48 tons
Maximum service speed:	80 or 90m.p.h.
E.E. engine brake hp:	1,470
Maximum tractive effort:	42,800 or 35,900lb.
Fuel tank capacity:	530gal.
Route availability:	5 (6 for 31/4s)

NEW PAINT — OLD NUMBERS

Plate 60 (above): In 1966, the first of the class appeared with a livery in accordance with British Rail's new 'corporate image'; all-over blue between full yellow ends. Although not unattractive when clean, it was not as pleasant as the original two-tone green. On 26th April 1973, No. 5635 passes Brentwood, with a boat train for Parkeston Quay, Harwich.

Brian Morrison

Plate 61 (right): Few instances have been recorded of a blue member of the class retaining the 'D' prefix to the number after repainting. Here No. 5860 hauls a Purfleet to Bevois Park (Southampton) freight past Purfleet Rifle Range, on 2nd March 1972.

Brian Morrison

Plate 62 (right): On a July day in 1973, No. 5530 prepares to rejoin the main Birmingham to Bristol line, at Lansdowne Junction, after traversing the Honeybourne branch, which is now closed to all forms of traffic. This Class 8 unfitted freight is made up of a bogie bolster wagon with steel bars, and a variety of loaded coal hoppers.
Barry J. Nicolle

Plate 63 (below): Retaining the green livery with all yellow ends, on 23rd July 1971, No. D5559 leads blue-liveried. No. 5845 through Doncaster with 'up' hoppers, and passes No. 5622, which has empty coaching stock. The pristine condition of the latter locomotive indicates that the new blue livery has only recently been applied at 'The Plant'.
Terry G. Flinders

Plate 64 (above): Shunting parcels vans alongside the main line, between Westbourne Park and Paddington, No. 5842 awaits departure of a Cardiff service from the terminus, before proceeding into the parcels bay, on 25th April 1973.
Brian Morrison

Plate 65 (right): Given a path over the 'up' main, a Class 7 freight trundles down Brentwood Bank, on 26th April 1973, powered by No. 5860.
Brian Morrison

Plate 66: An August 1972 scene, with No. 5682 leaving Chinnor to return to Princes Risborough after working a coal train to the Chinnor Cement Works, which can be seen in the background. The train is passing the site of Chinnor Station, which closed to passengers in July 1957 when the Watlington branch was removed from the timetable. The line remains open to a point just beyond the cement works return sidings, but for freight traffic only.

Geoff Gamble

Plate 67: In the spring of 1973, No. 5634 climbs the 1 in 103 gradient of Brentwood Bank towards Ingrave Summit with a delightful train of four-wheel ventilated vans and two parcels coaches, heading for Parkeston Quay at Harwich. By this time, all the class had received English Electric 12SVT engines, rated at 1,470b.h.p., in replacement for the original Mirrlees JVS12Ts which, after some half a million miles of running, began to show serious signs of stress. This was due, in all probability, to the upratings perpetrated upon them in their formative years. The original Mirrlees engines were all overhauled and sold off, and the majority are still in use today as marine power for a variety of trawlers.

Brian Morrison

THE KING'S CROSS COLLECTION

Page 68 (right): The Brush Type 2s and King's Cross were synonymous for many years, with the locomotives' almost exclusive use in and out of the terminus with both the local and semi-fast services, and the many empty coaching stock workings that were needed prior to introduction of the High Speed Trains. Late at night, on 5th November 1973, there are no fireworks from No. 5596, as it waits patiently to remove empty stock from the London terminus of the old Great Northern Railway.
Brian Morrison

Plate 69 (below): Empty coaching stock for a Humberside service, headed by No. 5608, bursts from Copenhagen Tunnel, on the run into King's Cross, on 22nd March 1973.
Brian Morrison

Plate 70: With Copenhagen Tunnel in the background, No. 5640 travels under the viaduct spanning Belle Isle, which carries the North London line. The locomotive is about to plunge into Gasworks Tunnel with empty stock to form an afternoon inter-city service for Leeds and Bradford.

Brian Morrison

Plate 71 (below): 1B66 was the code used for both 'up' and 'down' services between King's Cross and Cambridge, still known at the time as the 'Cambridge Buffet Expresses'. In March 1973, No. 5568 decends Holloway Bank and is about to enter Copenhagen Tunnel, on the final mile into the terminus. Sadly, this locomotive was the first of the class to be withdrawn from service, in October 1975, after being involved in an accident in Corby Tunnel, Northamptonshire. The accident involved a brake van and 38 coke wagons which ran loose and out of control away from the erstwhile British Steel Corporation's sidings at Corby and, at speed, hit the locomotive head on. The resulting damage to the locomotive was so extensive as to render it beyond economical repair.

Brian Morrison

Plate 72 (left): Empty coaching stock to form the 'Tees-Tyne Pullman' passes under the flyover that led into King's Cross Yard, prior to the many changes that have since been made in this area. In this view No. 5605 rolls easily down the 1 in 107 incline, on 12th September 1973.
Brian Morrison

Plate 74 (above right): The 16.50 Moorgate to Hertford (North) local train climbs through Holloway on a warm autumn evening in 1974, powered by No. 5599. The bodyside steps to the right of the cab have still to be plated over.
Brian Morrison

Plate 73 (below): The rationalisation of the tracks out of King's Cross, the demise of everything except multiple aspect signalling with the consequent demolition of the signal boxes, and the erection of overhead electrified wires, have all had a significant part to play in altering this scene almost out of recognition – even the church in the background has gone! On 22nd March 1973, No. 5612 climbs Holloway Bank with a load of roadstone from King's Cross Yard.
Brian Morrison

Plate 75 (below): All four distant signals remain firmly in the 'on' position, as No. 5652 passes slowly by with empty coaching stock that is to form the 16.25 King's Cross to Cleethorpes service.

Brian Morrison

PROGRAMMED

With the advent of British Rail's 'Total Operations Processing System', known as the T.O.P.S. computer, the number of each individual locomotive was changed to incorporate the class identification as the first two digits. Those that had, by this time, been re-engined were accorded the classification of 31, while those that were still fitted with the Mirrlees power unit were given the class number 30. By the time that the numbers were actually applied (1973), however, all the engine changing was complete and no locomotive actually carried a Class 30 designation. The original batch of locomotives still fitted with electro-magnetic control equipment were classified 31/0, the standard locomotives, 31/1, and the types fitted with electric train heating equipment became 31/4.

Original number	T.O.P.S. number	Subsequent change	Original number	T.O.P.S. number	Subsequent change
D5500	31018		D5521	31103	
D5501	31001		D5522	31104	31418
D5502	31002	ADB 968016	D5523	31105	
D5503	31003		D5524	31106	
D5504	31004		D5525	31107	
D5505	31005		D5526	31108	
D5506	31006	ADB 968017	D5527	31109	
D5507	31007		D5528	31110	
D5508	31008		D5529	31111	
D5509	31009		D5530	31112	
D5510	31010		D5531	31113	
D5511	31011		D5532	31114	
D5512	31012		D5533	31115	
D5513	31013	ADB 968013	D5534	31116	
D5514	31014	ADB 968015	D5535	31117	
D5515	31015		D5536	31118	
D5516	31016		D5537	31119	
D5517	31017		D5538	31120	
D5518	31101		D5539	31121	
D5519	31019		D5540	31122	
D5520	31102		D5541	31123	
			D5542	31124	
			D5543	31125	
			D5544	31126	
			D5545	31127	
			D5546	31128	
			D5547	31129	
			D5548	31130	
			D5549	31131	
			D5550	31132	
			D5551	31133	31450
			D5552	31134	
			D5553	31135	
			D5554	31136	
			D5555	31137	31444
			D5556	31138	
			D5557	31139	31438
			D5558	31140	31421
			D5559	31141	
			D5560	31142	

Plate 76: Cabside detail of Class 31/1 No. 31203 (ex-No. 5627), seen awaiting departure from King's Cross with a semi-fast train for Peterborough. Unaware of the camera, the driver, with hands clasped, could be uttering a prayer to the patron saint of ASLEF for a safe and happy journey!

Brian Morrison

Original number	T.O.P.S. number	Subsequent change	Original number	T.O.P.S. number	Subsequent change
D5561	31143		D5614	31191	
D5562	31144		D5615	31192	
D5563	31145		D5616	31406	
D5564	31146		D5617	31193	31426
D5565	31147		D5618	31194	31427
D5566	31148	31448	D5619	31195	
D5567	31149		D5620	31196	
D5568	31150		D5621	31197	31423
D5569	31151	31435	D5622	31198	
D5570	31152		D5623	31199	
D5571	31153	31432	D5624	31200	
D5572	31154		D5625	31201	
D5573	31155		D5626	31202	
D5574	31156		D5627	31203	
D5575	31157	31424	D5628	31204	31440
D5576	31158		D5629	31205	
D5577	31159		D5630	31206	
D5578	31160		D5631	31207	
D5579	31161		D5632	31208	
D5580	31162		D5633	31209	
D5581	31163		D5634	31210	
D5582	31164		D5635	31211	31428
D5583	31165		D5636	31212	
D5584	31166		D5637	31213	
D5585	31167		D5638	31214	
D5586	31168		D5639	31215	
D5587	31169		D5640	31407	
D5588	31170		D5641	31216	
D5589	31401		D5642	31217	
D5590	31171		D5643	31218	
D5591	31172	31420	D5644	31219	
D5592	31402		D5645	31220	31441
D5593	31173				
D5594	31174				
D5595	31175				
D5596	31403				
D5597	31176				
D5598	31177	31443			
D5599	31178				
D5600	31179	31436			
D5601	31180				
D5602	31181				
D5603	31182	31437			
D5604	31183				
D5605	31404				
D5606	31405				
D5607	31184				
D5608	31185				
D5609	31186				
D5610	31187				
D5611	31188				
D5612	31189				
D5613	31190				

Plate 77: Newly-adorned with the City of York crest above the number, No. 31406 is a Class 31/4 locomotive, but still retains the legend 31/1 on the cabside information panel, and shows a route availability number of 5, whereas all Class 31/4s are Code 6.

Brian Morrison

Original number	T.O.P.S. number	Subsequent change	Original number	T.O.P.S. number	Subsequent change
D5646	31408		D5805	31275	
D5647	31221		D5806	31276	
D5648	31222		D5807	31277	
D5649	31223		D5808	31278	
D5650	31224		D5809	31279	
D5651	31225		D5810	31280	
D5652	31226		D5811	31281	
D5653	31227		D5812	31413	
D5654	31228		D5813	31282	
D5655	31229		D5814	31414	
D5656	31409		D5815	31283	
D5657	31230		D5816	31284	
D5658	31231		D5817	31285	
D5659	31232		D5818	31286	
D5660	31233		D5819	31287	
D5661	31234		D5820	31288	
D5662	31235		D5821	31289	
D5663	31236	31433	D5822	31290	
D5664	31237		D5823	31291	
D5665	31238		D5824	31415	
D5666	31239	31439	D5825	31292	
D5667	31240		D5826	31293	
D5668	31241		D5827	31294	
D5669	31410		D5828	31295	31447
D5670	31242		D5829	31296	
D5671	31243		D5830	31297	
D5672	31244		D5831	31298	
D5673	31245		D5832	31299	
D5674	31246		D5833	31300	31445
D5675	31247		D5834	31301	
D5676	31248		D5835	31302	
D5677	31249		D5836	31303	
D5678	31250		D5837	31304	
D5679	31251	31442	D5838	31305	
D5680	31252		D5839	31306	
D5681	31253	31431	D5840	31307	31449
D5682	31254		D5841	31308	
D5683	31255		D5842	31416	
D5684	31256		D5843	31309	
D5685	31257		D5844	31310	31422
D5686	31258	31434	D5845	31311	
D5687	31259		D5846	31312	
D5688	31260		D5847	31313	
D5689	31261		D5848	31314	
D5690	31262		D5849	31315	
D5691	31411		D5850	31316	31446
D5692	31412		D5851	31317	
D5693	31263		D5852	31318	
D5694	31264		D5853	31319	
D5695	31265	31430	D5854	31320	
D5696	31266		D5855	31321	
D5697	31267	31419	D5856	31417	
D5698	31268		D5857	31322	
D5699	31269	31429	D5858	31323	
D5800	31270		D5859	31324	
D5801	31271		D5860	31325	
D5802	31272		D5861	31326	
D5803	31273		D5862	31327	
D5804	31274	31425			

PADDINGTON 'A' TURNS

Plate 78: At the same time as the Western Region was seeking to eliminate its fleet of diesel-hydraulic locomotives, a number of Class 31s became surplus to Eastern Region requirements, and were duly transferred. On 21st May 1975, No. 31118 has been rostered for the fairly heavy 15.05 Paddington to Hereford working, seen here slowly drawing away from the London terminus.

Brian Morrison

Plate 79: Hauling seven Mk. I coaches that comprise the 18.30 Paddington to Reading commuter express, No. 31304 passes under Ranelagh Bridge, on the exit from Paddington, on 21st May 1975.

Brian Morrison

Plate 80 (above): Nos. 31258 and 31259, in multiple, leave Paddington on 21st May 1975 hauling the 18.05 commuter service for Oxford, where it is timed to arrive at 19.12.

Brian Morrison

Plate 81 (below): With its BR symbol beneath the cabside number, instead of on the bodyside, No. 31258 is making an excellent job of maintaining time with this Paddington to Hereford express, as it races through Sonning Cutting, on the approaches to Reading, on 27th April 1974.

Brian Morrison

YORKSHIRE MISCELLANY

Plate 82 (above): Hauling a Class 9 unfitted coal train with a brake van on each end, No. 31148 passes through Selby Station, on 14th June 1974, and heads south.

Brian Morrison

Plate 83 (left): On 23rd November 1975, an engineer's train of ballast heads south through the magnificent portals of York Station, while rostered to No. 31218 which, at the time, was allocated to Finsbury Park Depot.

Brian Morrison

Plate 84: The Bradford portion of the 10.30 working from Paignton is taken out of Leeds, on 20th September 1975, by No. 31253. On the left, awaiting departure, can be seen Class 45 'Peak' No. 45020 with the 17.38 Leeds to Bristol service, and in the platform on the right is a Metro-Cammell Class 101 diesel multiple unit forming a stopping train for Huddersfield.

Brian Morrison

Plate 85: On 13th June 1974, No. 31287 ambles past Pilmoor, near Thirsk, and heads for Newcastle District with a freight comprising mainly coal hoppers.

Brian Morrison

EASTERN REGION 'A' TURNS

Plate 86 (above): Skegness Terminus, on the sunny afternoon of 14th June 1975. Awaiting its allotted hour, the 14.00 (SO) service for Chesterfield comprises nine bogies but is nevertheless, still entrusted to a Type 2 locomotive, Class 31 No. 31221 of Sheffield (Tinsley).
Stanley Creer

Plate 87 (below): On 10th August 1974, Finsbury Park Depot considered that two of the class were preferable for the eight bogies of the 09.25 (SO) King's Cross to Skegness working. In multiple, Nos. 31209 and 31222 ease the train through Sleaford.
Graham Wise

Plate 88: The last major modification to the class was the conversion, initially of 24 locomotives, to supply electric train heating for use on empty stock workings into King's Cross, with the new Mk. II air-conditioned stock which was equipped only for electric heating. Given the sub-division 31/4, these types are more fully described later in the album. On 6th December 1975, No. 31407 climbs to the summit of the 1 in 200 incline to Potters Bar, with the 13.30 King's Cross to Cambridge buffet service. These trains now run exclusively from Liverpool Street.

Brian Morrison

Plate 89: Passing through Tottenham Hale Station, in North London, No. 31239 is on time with the 14.36 Liverpool Street to King's Lynn express, on 21st February 1976.

Brian Morrison

FREIGHT CONTRASTS

Plate 90 (above): An unfitted Class 7 coal train for the London Midland Region from Herrington Colliery, County Durham, passes Darlington on the late evening of 12th June 1974, hauled by No. 31278.
Brian Morrison

Plate 91 (below): Passing Market Rasen, on 13th June 1975, a Barnetby to Sleaford ballast train is in the charge of No. 31327. This locomotive was the last of the 263 in the class to be constructed, in October 1962.
Stanley Creer

Plate 92: Somerset & Dorset Joint Railway Class 7F 2-8-0 locomotive, No. 53808, is towed away from Castle Cary, on 8th January 1976, en route from the Somerset & Dorset Society headquarters at Radstock to a new base on the West Somerset Railway.

Graham Scott-Lowe

Plate 93: A vintage scene at Horton-in-Ribblesdale, on the Settle & Carlisle line, on 14th June 1974, with No. 31123 in charge of the daily pick-up freight from Carlisle to Skipton.

Stanley Creer

Plate 94 (above): On 25th June 1975, No. 31269 throws exhaust into the air while starting away the 17.55 parcels train from Norwich for Ipswich. On the right, Class 37 No. 37017 has charge of the 18.40 service for Liverpool Street.

Brian Morrison

Plate 95 (below): Fruit vans for Norwich, from Fakenham, arrive at their destination on 25th June 1975, rostered to No. 31122. In the background, behind the locomotive, can be seen the five refuelling points that are used, in the main, by the prolific numbers of diesel multiple units that ply their trade about East Anglia.

Brian Morrison

IN THE 'SMOKE'

Plate 96: Emerging from the now-abandoned bore of Gasworks Tunnel, No. 31218 arrives at King's Cross, on 12th June 1975, with the 07.10 semi-fast service from Royston. The first blind of the four character headcode box has been broken, showing the bulbs behind that supply the illumination.

Brian Morrison

Plate 97 (right): A rake of post-war non-gangwayed outer suburban second class stock is brought into Farringdon, on 5th August 1976, to form an evening peak time working from Moorgate. The locomotive, No. 31222, has had a form of filler inserted into the gangway door surrounds, in an attempt to stop the draught that emanated from there when at speed.
John G. Glover

Plate 98 (below): Early morning activity at King's Cross, on a sunny June day in 1975. With empty coaching stock from the suburban platforms, No. 31199 heads for Gasworks Tunnel, and is caught by the camera above the roof of another set of empty carriage stock arriving to form an inter-city express for Leeds. In the main line platforms is another Class 31 with yet more empty coaching stock, and a Class 47 with an express for Newcastle.
Brian Morrison

Plate 99 (right): Heading the 09.30 semi-fast train for Cambridge away from King's Cross, on 12th June 1975, is e.t.h.-fitted Class 31/4 No. 31401, the first of the class to have the conversion, and originally numbered D5589.
Brian Morrison

Plate 100 (right): On 24th March 1975, No. 31249 waits at the Wood Green No. 1 box home signal for a path over the Hertford branch, where the empty coaching stock working (5A20) will set back into the washer, prior to storage in Hornsey Carriage Sidings. As No. D5677, this locomotive was the first to receive an English Electric engine in lieu of the original Mirrlees one. Passing to the rear of No. 31249 is No. 31198, with a King's Cross to Grange Park trip working.
Ken Brunt

MK. I HAULAGE

Plate 101: Working a rather onerous Type 4 diagram, with the 10.25 Birmingham (New Street) to Paddington service, No. 31294 rolls into Leamington Spa, on 14th September 1974, with seven well-laden Mk. I bogies.
Brian Morrison

Plate 102: Negotiating the Firsby curve with a similar haul, No. 31138 heads towards Skegness, on 14th June 1975, with the 12.15 ex-Leeds working. The abandoned trackbed behind the travel-stained disc-carrying locomotive once carried the Great Northern Railway through Louth, and also connected Skegness with Cleethorpes.
Stanley Creer

Plate 103: With the morning sun slowly dispersing an overnight mist, a 'down' excursion approaches Bury St. Edmunds, on 15th October 1977, behind No. 31125. This was another of the class constructed without the headcode box and, in consequence, is still using a disc code — albeit the wrong one in this instance!

Brian Morrison

Plate 104: The 12.30 King's Cross to Peterborough semi-fast train bursts from Potters Bar Tunnel, on 6th December 1975, powered by No. 31201.

Brian Morrison

THE 'SKINHEAD' VARIETY

Plate 105: Inevitably, to receive the nickname of 'Skinhead', the disc-carrying Class 31s are otherwise no different from the majority of the class. On 27th May 1978, the 06.33 Plymouth to Old Oak Common vans train descends from Crofton to Bedwyn, on the Berks & Hants line, and runs alongside the Kennet & Avon Canal behind No. 31134.

John Vaughan

Plate 106 (above): With three of the four discs displayed, No. 31117 brings a string of vans through Basingstoke from the Western Region on a very cold but sunny 3rd December 1977.

Brian Morrison

Plate 107 (below): Approaching Manningtree in Essex, on 19th May 1977, and passing the withdrawn 'Brighton Belle' Pullman unit No. 3053 in the sidings, No. 31133 is being utilised for haulage of an engineer's train.

Brian Morrison

Plate 108 (left): On 30th December 1977, No. 31138 passes Ipswich hauling the 11.52 (TThO) empty oil tank train from Norwich to Ripple Lane, Barking. Constant draught problems with the gangway doors has resulted in them being plated over with the resultant loss of two of the four front discs, making their use obsolete.
John C. Baker

Plate 109 (below): No. 31111 arrives at March East junction, on a sunny April day, with empty wagons bound for Whitemoor Yard.
Les Nixon

Plate 110 (left): Beneath the unsightly catenary supports that now infest the East Coast Main Line, from King's Cross to Welwyn, No. 31144 approaches Wood Green on 3rd June 1979 hauling empty coaching stock. The gangway doors still remain on this locomotive but are never used and, in fact, are believed to have been obsolete since the original trials took place with two of the class in multiple, as long ago as the late 1950s.
Brian Morrison

Plate 111 (below): With shovels flailing, and strangely reminiscent of an ancient slave ship, fresh ballast is deposited on the 'up' main line alongside Ripple Lane Yard. No. 31107 travels slowly but the team of men still have to work in a quite animated fashion to keep up and, despite a sunny but cold 19th November 1979, have no trouble keeping warm!
Brian Morrison

Plate 112: Freight traffic to and from the Ripple Lane Yards is quite diverse, but the majority emanates from the massive oil terminals at Coryton and Thames Haven on the Thames Estuary. On 31st October 1979, Nos. 31110 and 31112 draw away with oil tanks and head east, passing a Class 47 with a similar load.

Brian Morrison

ODD MAN OUT

Plate 113: No. 31418, formerly D5522, was unique among the Class 31/4 e.t.h.-fitted members of the class, in having 80m.p.h. gearing and no headcode box. Apart from this example, the 80m.p.h. series of electro-pneumatic Class 31s now runs from No. 31101 (formerly D5518) to 31116. Here, No. 31418 leaves Salisbury, on 17th April 1980, with the 10.10 Exeter (St. David's) to Waterloo working, subbing for a Class 33.

Andy French

Plate 114: Seemingly a warm summer day, but in fact this scene at Llanwern, between Newport and Severn Tunnel Junction, was recorded on 19th December 1979. Here, No. 31418 hauls a Cardiff to Portsmouth Harbour service, and passes Class 47/0 No. 47128 with a 'down' freight.

John Vaughan

'0000' AND VARIETIES

Plate 115 (above): The British Rail decision to abolish headcodes on all forms of motive power, except multiple units engaged in suburban services, resulted in the route indicator panels being set permanently to '0000', and the selector and operating handles being removed. This was an interim measure, prior to the fitting of marker lights. In this condition, No. 31314 pauses at Low Ellers Junction, on 6th February 1977, with a breakdown train.

Gavin Morrison

Plate 116 (right): At Farringdon, in the heart of the City of London, No. 31192 takes its empty stock to Moorgate for a peak time commuter service to North London, on 5th August 1976.

John G. Glover

Plate 117: At Treeton Junction, Tinsley (Sheffield) No. 31181 is nicely framed by the signals when passing with an 'up' freight on 28th February 1977. In the background is the test locomotive of the Class 47 fleet, then numbered 47601 but now 47901.

Les Nixon

Plate 118 (right): With vibration having resulted in the first '0' slowly becoming a '1', No. 31315 passes Kensington Olympia, on 24th March 1976, with a haul of steel bars from Hither Green to Whitemoor. The unfitted train is passing Class 33 'Slim Jim' Crompton No. 33205.
Brian Morrison

Plate 119 (below): Leaving Exeter (St. David's) on 13th July 1976, with the 09.55 train for Newton Abbot, No. 31112 displays its row of 0s in a diagonal fashion. The old water-tower on the left has since been demolished.
Brian Morrison

Plate 120 (above): With a headcode seemingly unique to itself, No. 31258 races through Southall, in West London, on 20th March 1976 hauling inter-city stock bound for Paddington. This was a very uncommon occurrence at the time, probably caused by the failure of a type 4 locomotive.

Brian Morrison

Plate 121 (below): With four neat dots in lieu of the usual 0s, No. 31311, in multiple with No. 31308, hauls 28 loaded 20 ton coke hopper wagons past Rotherham Road box, on 2nd June 1977.

Gavin Morrison

Plate 122: Despite the weak sunlight prevailing on 15th January 1977, the temperature was only just above freezing point as e.t.h.-fitted Class 31/4 No. 31407 approaches Finsbury Park with the eight coach 13.05 King's Cross to Peterborough semi-fast train.

Brian Morrison

Plate 123: With an identical haul, No. 31235 passes under the M62 motorway at Brighouse, Yorkshire, with the 'summer Saturdays only' service from Bridlington to Bradford, on 16th September 1978.

Gavin Morrison

Plate 124: Where six bridge openings were once needed only one survives today, this being for the two remaining tracks that pass through Brighouse; a sad reminder of the ever-decreasing railway dominance in this country. In this view, photographed on 24th July 1976, the 08.50 Weymouth to Bradford Saturday service is headed by No. 31325.

Gavin Morrison

Plate 125: A few Class 31/4s spent a period allocated to Cricklewood Depot in the mid-1970s, being used in the main for empty stock working from St. Pancras. Why Immingham-based No. 31113 was on Cambridge Street Fuelling Depot, just outside St. Pancras, on 9th March 1978 is, however not known. Class 47/4 Co-Co No. 47491 is the other, more normal, occupant. This fuelling point is now almost derelict, following the introduction of High Speed Trains on the Midland main line, which have no need of such a facility.

Brian Morrison

MARKER LIGHTS

Plate 126: As members of the class passed through Doncaster Works for overhaul, the blinds were removed from the roof-mounted boxes and marker lights were put in their place. With its 'new look' front end, No. 31290 curves through the platforms at Bath Spa, on 24th September 1982, hauling freight.

Brian Morrison

Plate 127 (above): On 20th August 1982, No. 31255 hurries past the closed station of Claydon, north of Ipswich, with the 08.18 Peterborough to Harwich train. Although the station closed in June 1963, the signal box at this time was still operational.

Colin J. Marsden

Plate 128 (below): Having emerged from Hadley South Tunnel, No. 31318 passes through Hadley Wood Station, on 3rd June 1979, with a Sunday engineer's train.

Brian Morrison

Plate 129 (right): With a haul of coal for Tinsley Yard, Sheffield, No. 31271 restarts from the home signal, between Kiveton Park and Kiveton Bridge, on 13th December 1979.
Colin J. Marsden

Plate 130 (below): Passing Bathampton, on 12th January 1983, a 'down' engineer's train approaches Bath Spa in the charge of No. 31217.
Brian Morrison

Plate 131 (above): The 'summer Saturdays' 07.08 Chesterfield to Yarmouth holiday train passes Heath Crossing, on 26th July 1980, powered by No. 31322, which was one of thirteen of the class allocated to York Depot at the time.

John C. Baker

Plate 132 (below): With the station footbridge at Pilning visible in the distance, No. 31291 approaches Severn Tunnel, on 9th June 1982, with a 'down' air-braked service (A.B.S.) freight. It took around twelve years to complete the 4 mile 628 yard tunnel under the Severn Estuary, and saved some 26 route miles for traffic when compared with the route via Gloucester.

Brian Morrison

E.T.H. FITTED

Plate 133 (above): The last major modification to some members of the class was the conversion to supply electric train heating, creating the sub-class of 31/4. Initially fitted to 24 of the class, seemingly picked at random from those that happened to be in for overhaul at the time, they were intended for use with the new electric-only Mk. II air-conditioned stock, newly operating from King's Cross. Introduction of High Speed Trains allowed for transfer elsewhere, and here No. 31410 is pictured, on the Settle & Carlisle line, heading a four coach Leeds to Carlisle service.

David Wilcock

Plate 134 (below): On 12th June 1982, No. 31422 winds into the platforms at Fareham, Hampshire, with the 14.10 Portsmouth Harbour to Cardiff (Central) service. The tracks straight ahead are for freight use only and terminate near Fort Brockhurst, the one-time junction for branch lines to Stokes Bay and to Lee-on-the-Solent.

Brian Morrison

28

Plate 135: (above): On the very wet evening of 22nd September 1982, No. 31420 prepares to move away from Weston-super-Mare with the 16.20 local service for Bristol (Temple Meads).

Brian Morrison

Plate 136 (below): With the removable roof hatches being put on upside down, both locomotives give the appearance of having a type of roof cowling, but this is not the case. On 10th September 1983, Nos. 31401 and 31417, both of the original batch of 24 e.t.h.-fitted locomotives, approach Trowse Swingbridge Junction, Norwich, with the 10.15 Birmingham (New Street) to Norwich service.

Brian Morrison

Plate 137 (left): Empty stock of the 00.05 Edinburgh to King's Cross sleeper train climbs out of Copenhagen Tunnel, on 8th June 1977, behind No. 31422. For the most part, the Class 31/4s retained their steam-heating facility in operational condition or isolated, thereby becoming dual-heated, dual-braked and multiple-controlled. The result is that they have more hoses and jumper cables jostling for space on their buffer beams than any other class of BR locomotive!
Brian Morrison

Plate 138 (below): Now the Class 31/4s are a regular performer on the Norwich to Birmingham services, No. 31423 approaches Leicester past the old Midland Railway North box, on 26th March 1983, heading the 09.49 ex-Norwich working.
Brian Morrison

Plate 139 (above): Class 31/4 No. 31419 comes to a halt at the curved platforms of Bath Spa, on 25th September 1982, with the 08.15 Cardiff (Central) to Portsmouth Harbour train, and is on time at 09.27, with arrival on the south coast scheduled for 11.45. In the other direction, Class 33/0 No. 33004 restarts the 06.56 Portsmouth Harbour to Bristol (Temple Meads) train.

Brian Morrison

Plate 140 (below): A nostalgic look at the old well-known signal gantry at Southampton, which has since been made a casualty of multiple aspect signalling. Coming beneath with the 08.56 Portsmouth Harbour to Bristol (Temple Meads) service, on 13th May 1978, is e.t.h.-fitted No. 31420.

Brian Morrison

Plate 141: A string of ten 12 ton shock-absorbing ventilated vans, known as 'Shock Partos', run down Ashley Bank, north of Bristol, on 15th July 1980 behind No. 31423.

John Vaughan

Plate 142: With very little evidence remaining that this was once the site of Armley Moor Station, No. 31409 passes by providing the motive power for the 13.08 King's Cross to Bradford inter-city service, on 21st June 1977.

Gavin Morrison

Plate 143: The passing of the ways at Dawlish Warren, on 16th July 1981, with No. 31420 heading the 17.15 Exeter (St. David's) to Paignton service, and Class 45 'Peak' No. 45062 approaching with the 16.37 Paignton to Exeter return.
Brian Morrison

Plate 144: Shortly after completion of the new track and tunnel layout at Holloway, No. 31404 crosses the rebuilt flyover, on 8th June 1977, with empty coaching stock to form the 09.00 King's Cross to Newcastle express.
Brian Morrison

A STRIPED COMPROMISE

Plate 145 (above): The original livery for the class, that included two wrap-round body stripes, was the most attractive ever carried. In the late 1970s, some Finsbury Park-allocated locomotives appeared with a silver stripe where the upper white/light green one used to be. The result was quite pleasing but destined not to last, although some Western Region-allocated members of the class did follow suit. On 26th September 1979, No. 31411, with the livery modifications, passes Wood Green heading for the Hertford North loop with empty stock.

Brian Morrison

Plate 146 (below): Carrying larger than normal numbers, in addition to the body stripe adornment, No. 31413 moves away from Bristol (Temple Meads), on 9th June 1982, with a van train.

Brian Morrison

Plate 147 (above): A rural scene at Whitlingham Junction, between Norwich and Brundall Gardens, on 24th August 1980, with '1 hp' vying for attention with 1,470 hp, as No. 31404 makes tracks for Yarmouth with an excursion from Stevenage!

John C. Baker

Plate 148 (below): Rostered for the lightweight 10.30 Gloucester to Swindon parcels train, No. 31415 ambles away from Standish Junction and approaches Stonehouse, on 15th July 1980.

John Chalcraft

Plate 149 (right): A fine bird's-eye view of Edinburgh (Waverley), on 27th May 1981, as No. 31405 moves away with the 13.25 service to Newcastle. It was only members of the sub-class 31/4 that received the body stripe.
Les Nixon

Plate 150 (right): With ballast from King's Cross Yard, No. 31403 climbs Holloway Bank, on 2nd June 1982, with a 'down' engineer's train.
Brian Morrison

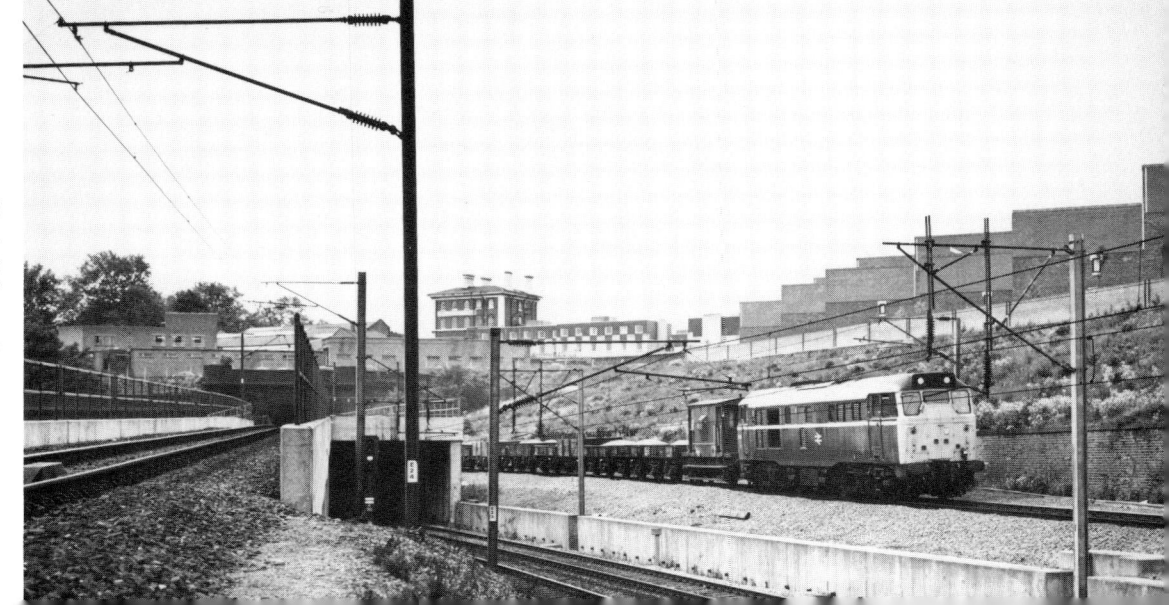

Plate 151: The stretch of old Midland Railway metals between Stamford and Peterborough once contained stations at Bainton Gate, Uffington, Helpston and Walton but, today, none of these remain to halt the progress of No. 31402, seen passing Helpston, on 16th August 1980, with the 11.50 Leicester to Peterborough service.

John C. Baker

Plate 152: Two striped examples of Class 31/4 locomotives, Nos. 31415 and 31416 hammer through Slough, on 3rd August 1981, double-heading a heavy ten bogie Paddington to Newbury train.

Barry Edwards

SNOWPLOUGHS — BUT NO SNOW

Plate 153: A few members of the class are fitted with small snowploughs at both ends, as in the case illustrated here of No. 31270 taking the new 'down' side route into Carr Yard, Doncaster, with mixed freight on 13th April 1981. The ploughs are often removed during the summer months and may, or may not, be restored to the same locomotive.
Les Nixon

Plate 154 (right): Hauling just two 'Grainflow Polybulks', on 22nd February 1984, No. 31304 comes off the Greenford branch at West Ealing, in West London, and heads eastwards. The shine on both track and sleepers betrays the fact that the photograph was taken in pouring rain.
Brian Morrison

Plate 155 (below): On a warm April evening in 1980, disc-carrying No. 31111 passes Manningham Junction box as it leaves Valley Road Goods Yard, Bradford, with the 18.10 freight working for Healey Mills.
John S. Whiteley

Plate 156 (right): On 12th August 1981, No. 31263 speeds through West Ealing with the 17.25 vans train from Bristol to Old Oak Common. The locomotive is still fitted with the outside ploughs, but the centre one is missing.
Colin J. Marsden

Plate 157 (right): Also without the centre plough No. 31319 approaches Wakefield (Kirkgate), on 5th January 1981, with freight from Leeds (Hunslet) to Healey Mills.
Bert Wynn

SNOW — BUT NO SNOWPLOUGHS!

Plate 158: Pre-Christmas snowfall is uncommon in the West Country, but it certainly occurred in 1981. Here, on 11th December, No. 31123 gets to grips with the icy rails with a short Freightliner train bound for Bristol (West) Depot.
John Chalcraft

Plate 159 (right): On 11th December 1981, No. 31419 has need of its heating facilities as it climbs Ashley Down Bank at Lockleaze, Bristol, with the 13.15 Portsmouth Harbour to Cardiff (Central) service.
Ian Gould

Plate 160: A bleak winter landscape at Skipton, Yorkshire, on 12th February 1983. In the platform is a BR Derby-built Class 108 diesel multiple unit, forming the 09.19 Morcambe to Leeds service. On the centre road, to the right, is a similar unit awaiting its next turn of duty and held on the through road is No. 31118, with a 'down' coal train.
Brian Morrison

Plate 161: Charging through a snow-covered Long Preston Station, between Hellifield and Settle Junction, a blizzard rages around No. 31410, on 8th February 1983, as it is photographed with the 08.57 Leeds to Carlisle service.
Brian Morrison

Plate 162: On 27th January 1979, 31174 passes Guiseley Junction at Shipley, Yorkshire, with parcels vans for Bradford (Forster Square). The combination of semaphore signals, a clean locomotive, snow and sunshine has resulted in perfect photographic conditions — providing one can put up with cold feet!

John S. Whiteley

Plate 163 (left): During the last six months of the 1,500V d.c. Woodhead route utilisation, No. 31116 eases a train of vanfits for Barnsley away from Barnsley Junction, Penistone, on 25th February 1981. Apart from having its T.O.P.S. number reproduced in the marker light panel, this locomotive is also non-standard in that no steps have been cut into the plate that has replaced the gangway doors, unlike the majority of other members of the class.

John Chalcraft

Plate 164 (below): Snow came early to East Anglia in 1980 and, on 29th November, No. 31318 runs down Bentley Bank, south of Ipswich, at the head of a short engineer's train.

Michael J. Collins

WEED-KILLERS

Plate 165 (above): A most uncommon photograph, showing a member of the class at work on a preserved line whilst the locomotive is still in British Rail stock. On 5th May 1982, No. 31131 is used on the Merryfield Lane extension of the East Somerset Railway to spray weed-killing chemicals from the Chipmans weed-killer train. This train, consisting of two ex-Southern Region coaches and a number of chemical tanks, is owned and operated by Chipman's men from Horsham in Surrey.
Ron Cover

Plate 166 (below): Apart from the Chipman's and Fisons' weed-killing trains, British Rail also operate one of their own, utilising an old wooden-bodied Gresley brake composite as the spray coach. Headed by No. 31200, the train is seen here working at Newark.
Geoff Dowling

THE PLANT

Plate 167 (above): A second batch of Class 31/1s commenced conversion for e.t.h. in late 1983. With the Trans-Pennine diesel multiple units being withdrawn after twenty four years in service, the Hull to Manchester trains were taken over by Class 31/4s at the commencement of the 1984 summer timetable. These locomotives can be distinguished from the earlier batch by their painted blue marker light panel boxes, as shown in this photograph of No. 31153 receiving a general overhaul in Doncaster Works, from where it emerged as No. 31432.
Colin J. Marsden

Plate 168 (right): Inside 'The Plant', on 10th August 1980, 'Skinhead' No. 31105 is the recipient of a major overhaul.
Brian Morrison

Plate 169 (above): Another example of a member of the class which has its number included as part of the marker light panel. No. 31276 is on jacks, with the bogies removed, undergoing a general repair inside 'The Plant' on 10th August 1980.

Brian Morrison

Plate 170 (right): Awaiting attention outside the Works, is Immingham-based No. 31248. This locomotive was one of just five of the class that received single line token equipment, of the type used in the Highlands of Scotland but, in this case, for the much more mundane single track iron-ore branch from High Dyke, near Grantham. The recess for the equipment has now been plated over.

Brian Morrison

IN TANDEM

Plate 171: Between East Somerset Junction (Witham) and Blatchbridge Junction (Frome), on 24th September 1982, Nos. 31170 and 31118 pass by with a permanent way train.

Brian Morrison

Plate 172: One of very few visits by the class to Waterloo was recorded on 28th March 1979, when a school special from Sherborne in Dorset arrived at the London terminus worked by No. 31210, leading No. 31271.

Colin J. Marsden

Plate 173: On a very hot 4th September 1980, Nos. 31201 and 31130 course down the Midland main line, on the approaches to Chesterfield, with a very neat load of fourteen rail tanks.

Brian Morrison

Plate 174: The space that contained the gangway doors on No. 31148 has been plated over and sealed up in non-standard fashion, with both foot rests and handrail being omitted, and the plate itself recessed some 2 in. into the front end. The locomotive is photographed under a threatening sky, on 11th September 1980, coupled to No. 31234 in Mark's Tey Sand Sidings with the daily sand train to Mile End, in East London.

Michael J. Collins

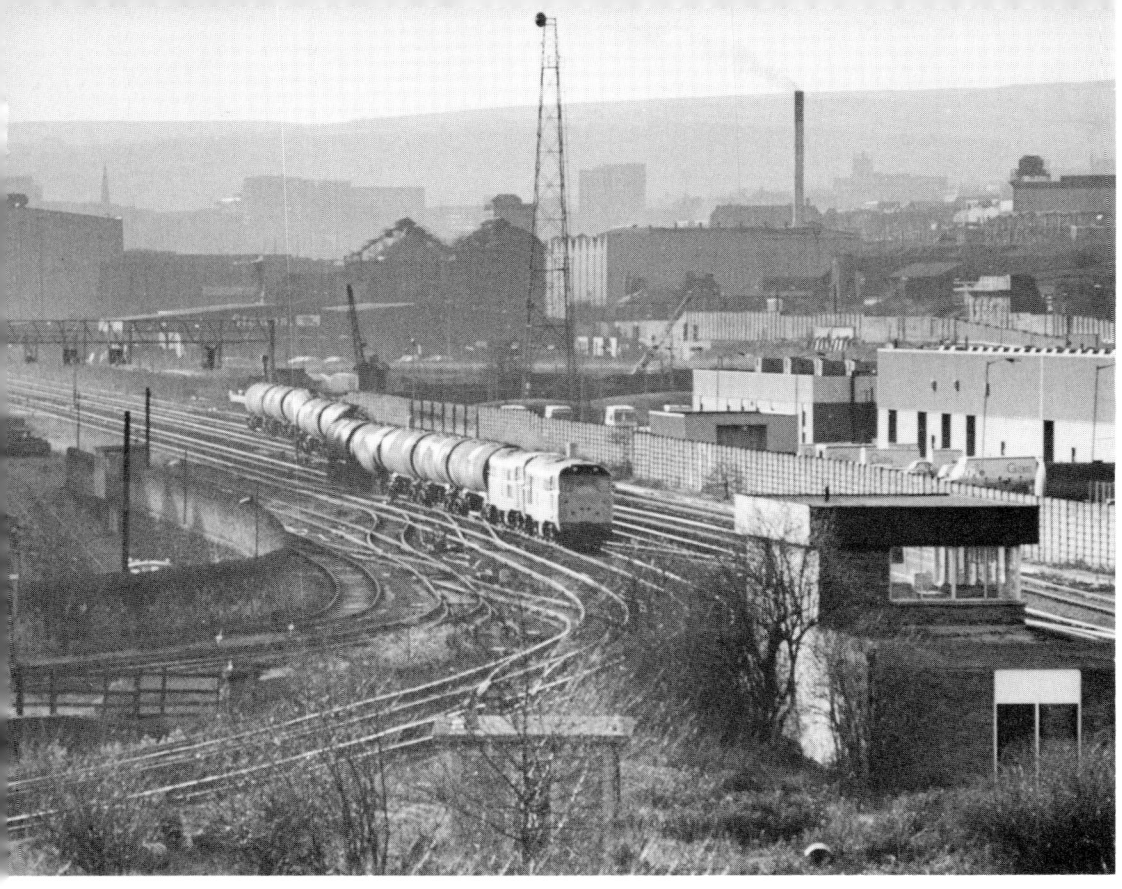

Plate 175 (left): Winding across the complicated pointwork at Brightside Junction, between Sheffield and Rotherham, on 10th December 1983, Nos. 31307 and 31301 turn off the main line and head for Tinsley Yard.

Brian Morrison

Plate 176 (below): Threading through the lush Avon Valley, near Freshford, on 22nd August 1981, Nos. 31159 and 31307 work in multiple while hauling the 16.10 Portsmouth Harbour to Cardiff (Central) train.

John Vaughan

FREIGHTLINERS

Plate 177 (above): On 22nd June 1979, No. 31206 surprisingly turned up with the 18.45 (SX) Freightliner service from Felixstowe and here passes Orwell, on the Felixstowe branch, and heads for Ipswich. Here the train will become part of the 21.24 (SX) Parkeston Quay to Edge Hill A.B.S. service, and will eventually set down at Trafford Park, Manchester.
John C. Baker

Plate 178 (below): Another rare occasion when a member of the class was utilised for a Freightliner working was recorded by the camera on 9th September 1980, when a Felixstowe to Parkeston Quay transfer working was placed in the hands of No. 31243, seen passing Mistley on the Harwich branch.
Michael J. Collins

HOLIDAY TRAFFIC

Plate 179: Passing Black Bank, on the line from Ely to March, on 5th September 1981, No. 31293 passes a harvesting scene with the eleven coach 09.57 (SO) Yarmouth to Manchester (Piccadilly) working — a particularly difficult roster for a Type 2 locomotive.

John C. Barker

Plate 180: On 30th August 1980, No. 31279 takes the Wainfleet curve in very gingerly fashion after leaving Skegness with the 11.37 (SO) return holiday train bound for Sheffield. Note the check rails on the track.

Brian Morrison

Plate 181: Summer Saturdays at Scarborough bring into the seaside town a variety of locomotives and trains, with holiday-makers from many parts of the country. At other times, all that is to be seen is a procession of diesel multiple units. Here, on 2nd August 1980, No. 31327 prepares to take the 11.10 departure to Sheffield.

Gavin Morrison

Plate 182: On a summer Saturday in 1980, No. 31128 restarts the heavy 08.55 Weymouth to Leeds train away from Basingstoke.

Andy French

Plate 183: Passing over the crossing at West Street Junction, No. 31219 slows for the Boston stop, on 30th August 1980, while hauling the 08.15 (SO) Peterborough to Skegness service.

Brian Morrison

Plate 184: The external cleanliness of the Bristol (Bath Road) allocation of e.t.h.-fitted members of the class has often left much to be desired, and here, a rather typical example leaves the train shed at Frome, on 7th June 1980, with the 16.14 Bristol (Temple Meads) to Weymouth service. Since this photograph was taken, the overall station roof, that dates back to the days of the GWR broad gauge, has been completely renovated.

John Chalcraft

Plate 185 (left): With the environs of Halifax looking just as one may imagine them, No. 31298 heads away from the town station with the summer (SO) 11.30 Bridlington to Bradford (Exchange) return holiday train.

John S. Whiteley

Plate 186 (below): With the mill at Heckington dominating the background, No. 31248 gallops through the station, on 14th July 1979, with another summer Saturday holiday train, the 08.38 Chesterfield to Skegness working. This location is on the Sleaford to Boston line.

Les Nixon

WEST COUNTRY SCENES

Plate 187: The well-known view from the sea wall at Teignmouth, but featuring a most unusual train for the location. On 29th August 1978, a pair of Class 31/1s round the curve from the station hauling ballast, heading in the direction of Exeter. The leading locomotive is No. 31151 working in multiple with No. 31135, both being allocated to March Depot, in the heart of Cambridgeshire, at this time!

Graham Scott-Lowe

Plate 188 (right): Passing Dawlish, on 8th April 1982, another pair of the class work in multiple on a southbound empty stock working, with No. 31128 heading No. 31291.

Bert Wynn

Plate 189: In a particularly attractive setting, on the approach to Cowley Bridge Junction, Exeter, No. 31420 brings the 16.45 Barnstaple to Newton Abbot Sunday service off the Barnstaple branch on 21st June 1981.

Barry Edwards

Plate 190 (right): A few trials took place in Cornwall to ascertain the acceptability of the class for china clay workings, but they were found to be too large for some of the china clay branches and the work was put into the hands of the Class 25s, and later, the Class 37s. Otherwise, appearances in the Duchy are almost unknown and it was a considerable surprise when No. 31173 came through Bodmin Road Station (now Bodmin Parkway) running 'light engine' back to Plymouth (Laira), after delivery of an early morning fruit train to St. Blazey, on the morning of 3rd June 1981.

John Hicks

Plate 191: (above) About to pass the fine old GWR signal box of Newton Abbot East, on 2nd July 1979, No. 31136 arrives at Newton Abbot with the 11.08 Paignton to Exeter (St. David's) local service.
Brian Morrison

Plate 192 (right): Just one freight working per day is booked for the Barnstaple branch, the 08.50 pick-up from Barnstaple to Exeter (Riverside) Yard. On 20th September 1983, No. 31190 jogs down the singled line near Bishop's Tawton, between Barnstaple and Chapelton.
Brian Morrison

Plate 193 (below): The Saturday 09.00 Weymouth to Bristol (Temple Meads) working is rostered for an e.t.h.-fitted Class 31/4 on 28th March 1981, and here No. 31421 awaits departure from the busy platforms of Yeovil (Pen Mill).
John Chalcraft

Plate 194 (above): The end house of St. John Street at Bridgwater, in Somerset would seem to be an ideal one for a railway enthusiast. Passing the station, on 23rd September 1982, No. 31117 clatters over the points with 'up' vans.

Brian Morrison

Plate 195 (below): The 09.11 Weymouth to Bristol (Temple Meads) local service, having left the single track at Castle Cary, enjoys a run up the Berks & Hants line, just east of Clink Road Junction, Frome, on 10th November 1979 behind Class 31/4 No. 31424.

John Vaughan

ON THE SETTLE & CARLISLE

Plate 196: In 1982, the Nottingham to Glasgow services via the Settle & Carlisle route were withdrawn by British Rail, and a Leeds to Carlisle substitute was put into the timetable calling at the only two stations left open on the route; Settle Junction and Appleby. A number of locomotive types were utilised including Classes 47, 45, 40, 31 and 25 although it was the Class 31s that appeared the most suited to the line, and they became the most common type to be seen on the service. On 2nd August 1982, No. 31117 crosses Ribblehead Viaduct in a morning mist, with the 08.57 Leeds to Carlisle train.

Ron Cover

Plate 197: Hauling the same train, on 18th February 1983, No. 31410 threads through the cutting at Blea Moor.

David Wilcock

Plate 198 (above): With the snow-capped peak of Ingleborough dominating the background, an ex-Finsbury Park locomotive, No. 31404, still retains its body stripe on 2nd April 1983, and again is captured with the 08.57 Leeds to Carlisle service passing Blea Moor signal box. Two Class 40s, Nos. 40129 and 40082, are in the standby loop to cover the great many West Coast Main Line diversions that traversed the Settle and Carlisle line on this Saturday, due to engineering works on their usual route.

David Wilcock

Plate 199 (below): Running downhill from Ais Gill Summit, on 5th April 1980, a twelve bogie 'Footex' special from Chesterfield to Carlisle requires a pair of Class 31/1s, in this case Nos. 31270 and 31246.

John S. Whiteley

Plate 200 (left): The reason why the 08.57 Leeds to Carlisle train appears to be photographed so often is that it is the only booked 'down' service on the Settle & Carlisle route to run during the hours of winter daylight! In this scene, photographed on 7th February 1983, No. 31410 passes Selside, near Ribblehead.
Brian Morrison

Plate 201 (below): On a bitingly cold January 1983 morning, the same train kicks up the snow, as the Class 31 at its head powers by Blea Moor hauling six Mk. I bogies.
David Wilcock

Plate 202: A superb photograph, and one that typifies a winter's morning on the beautiful Settle & Carlisle line. On 7th February 1983, No. 31410 (a regular performer at this time) passes a pair of hardy gangers who are engaged in track maintenance at Blea Moor.

David Wilcock

Plate 203: Not strictly on the line from Settle to Carlisle, but approaching it at a spot between Hellifield and Long Preston, on 12th February 1983, No. 31411, with the more normal five bogies, heads the morning service northwards towards Carlisle.

Brian Morrison

EREWASH VALLEY FREIGHT

Plate 204 (right): The route from Trent Junction to Clay Cross Junction, crossing the Derbyshire/Yorkshire border, is popularly known as the Erewash Valley line. It is primarily used for freight services but does see some passenger traffic; that which is required to service the station at Alfreton & Mansfield Parkway. On 14th April 1981, Nos. 31153 and 31130 pass Toton Yard with 'down' bogie bolster wagons.

John S. Whiteley

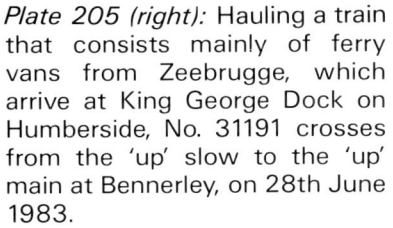

Plate 205 (right): Hauling a train that consists mainly of ferry vans from Zeebrugge, which arrive at King George Dock on Humberside, No. 31191 crosses from the 'up' slow to the 'up' main at Bennerley, on 28th June 1983.

Brian Morrison

Plate 206 (right): On 28th June 1983, a surprise appearance was made, at Trowell Junction, by a rake of 1938 red-liveried London Transport Executive underground stock! On its final journey to the scrap-yard in the Rotherham/Sheffield area, it is sandwiched between two London Transport brake vans that are adapted to couple at their inner ends to the electric multiple unit's automatic couplers. The unusual looking result is hauled very carefully by No. 31306.

Brian Morrison

Plate 207 (left): A very heavy train of large bogie tanks runs down the Erewash Valley, near Heanor South, on 19th June 1980, powered by Nos. 31284 and 31278, both of Thornaby Depot.

John Vaughan

Plate 208 (left): Approaching Alfreton & Mansfield Parkway, on 29th June 1983, with empty bogie bolsters returning to Tinsley (Sheffield), Nos. 31224 and 31238 work in multiple and produce around 2,940b.h.p.

Brian Morrison

Plate 209 (left): Powering through Clay Cross Junction with a train of steel coil, Nos. 31203 and 31276 head southwards for Trent Junction, on 30th June 1983. The twin tracks on the left lead to Derby, via Ambergate South Junction and Duffield

Brian Morrison

THREE-UP!

Plate 210: A number of double-headed trains are the result of a failure of the rostered locomotive, with another being found to take the original engine and load on to their destination. Where the substitute power is a pair of locomotives working in multiple, the result is triple-heading, as depicted on the next two pages. At a time when they were popularly known as Taunton's 'terrible twins', Nos. 31170 and 31128 haul failed Class 45/0 'Peak' No. 45068 into Taunton Station, after the latter had failed on the York to Newton Abbot Motorail train of 26th July 1980. The two Class 31s have long since been parted, and are currently allocated to Bescot and Cricklewood respectively.

John Vaughan

Plate 211 (left): On 26th January 1982, Nos. 31308 and 31133 give assistance to Class 47/4 No. 47420, seen on a northbound freight passing through Burton upon Trent.

Bert Wynn

Plate 212: Class 31s haul the 'Cornish Riviera'! With one of the two power cars of a Class 253 High Speed Train not working properly, Nos. 31307 and 31314 are attached to the front of the 'down' express, on 1st May 1982, in order to give much-needed assistance over the South Devon banks ahead.

Andy French

Plate 213: On 28th June 1983, the new Class 58 Co-Co No. 58002 was provided, for its first revenue-earning trip, with a Toton to Corby freight, and return. As an insurance against 'teething troubles' with the new locomotive, a Class 56 was coupled inside the Class 58 to provide power if necessary but, in fact, the Class 56 failed! A pair of Class 31s, Nos. 31224 and 31238, took its place, and the ensemble was photographed passing Normanton on Soar, north of Loughborough, with the return working for Toton.

Brian Morrison

IN THE NORTH EAST

Plate 214 (left): At the point where the elevated section of the A19 trunk road spans both the River Tees and Tees Yard at Thornaby, No. 31284 makes tracks for Redcar Steelworks, on 27th May 1980, with empty bogie bolster wagons that will be used here for transportation of steel coil. This locomotive is still fitted with a steam lance in the standard position, beneath the buffer beam, despite icy conditions being rather uncommon at this time of the year! Normally steam lances are fitted only to Class 47s and 31s, as dictated by weather conditions, and are normally removed again after use. They work, of course, from the locomotive's steam heat boiler.
Brian Morrison

Plate 215 (below): Heading south from Durham, across the viaduct that dominates the town from nearly every aspect, a mixed freight, consisting mainly of steel, is dragged high above the rooftops, on 27th May 1980, by No. 31287, then allocated to Thornaby (Tees), but currently a Midlands locomotive from Bescot.
Brian Morrison

Plate 216 (left): Having run round their train, Nos. 31318 and 31207 await departure from Whitby, on 9th October 1981, as the second man takes the tail lamp to the rear of the train. This is another instance where the removable roof hatch has been put on upside down, giving the impression that the leading locomotive has a roof cowl of sorts.
John Chalcraft

Plate 217 (left): Having just crossed Chester le Street Viaduct, No. 31264 growls towards the station on a dull May evening in 1980 while hauling an 'up' mixed, unfitted freight.
Brian Morrison

Plate 218 (below): Heading away from Berwick-upon-Tweed and passing Redshin Cove, No. 31217 skirts the North Sea coast, on the evening of 10th June 1978, in charge of the 17.15 Edinburgh to Newcastle service.
Les Nixon

WELSH WORKINGS

Plate 219 (above): Currently, no Class 31 locomotives are allocated to Welsh motive power depots, but they are still regular performers in Wales on a variety of duties. On 13th March 1982, No. 31122 crosses the River Usk at low tide, leaving Newport with a Saturday afternoon 'up' parcels vans service, consisting of some fifteen bogies.

John S. Whiteley

Plate 220 (below): On 9th June 1982, No. 31401 scurries past Pwll-Mawr, on the outskirts of Cardiff, making light work of the five Mk. I coaches that form the 18.00 service from Cardiff (Central) to Portsmouth Harbour.

Brian Morrison

Plate 221: Leaving Cardiff behind, and passing Pengam Junction, in June 1982, No. 31228 speeds express parcels vans for Bristol past Roath Goods Sidings. The lines at the top left of the picture lead to Tidal Yard and Cardiff Docks.
Brian Morrison

Plate 222: A block working of chemical tanks passes Llanwern, on 20th June 1979, behind Nos. 31213 and 31231, which are seen working in multiple. Llanwern lies between Newport and Severn Tunnel Junction, and the lines to the right lead to the Llanwern Steelworks of the British Steel Corporation.
Graham Scott-Lowe

THE CAMBRIDGE LINE

Plate 223: Passing the rather rustic ambience of Stanstead in Essex, No. 31112 passes the station, on 28th July 1981, with the 17.26 Cambridge to Liverpool Street semi-fast service.

Colin J. Marsden

Plate 224: Until September 1952, Elsenham was the junction for the branch to Thaxted, but little remains to indicate the fact today. However, the original station buildings survive and there are still manually-controlled crossing gates, despite being on a main line. Here No. 31112 rolls the 15.36 Liverpool Street to Cambridge train into the station.

Colin J. Marsden

Plate 225: Heading the 13.36 Liverpool Street to Cambridge buffet service, No. 31205 bursts from the northern portal of Audley End Tunnel, Essex, on 14th September 1978.

Les Nixon

Plate 226: Passing Shelford Station, just south of Shepreth Branch Junction, No. 31160 heads towards Cambridge with a permanent way train consisting, primarily, of concrete sleepers, in June 1981. Prior to the T.O.P.S. renumbering, this locomotive was No. D5578, one of two of the class that received an experimental livery. Probably a harbinger of the yellow warning panel, this locomotive was painted in unlined light blue, with No. D5579 being turned out in a sort of light golden ochre. After some time they were, however, returned to a standard livery.

Brian Morrison

Plate 227: Given the very onerous task of keeping time with the ten coach 09.25 King's Lynn to Liverpool Street express, No. 31261 is only a few minutes late departing from Cambridge on 29th September 1978. With some spirited running, of which this locomotive is capable, it has a good chance of reaching the London terminus on time, despite this being a Type 3 or Type 4 diagram. It is worthy of note that this particular locomotive is still fitted with its original gangway doors, which have been welded up instead of having a new plate fitted. Therefore, the hinge mounts are still showing and the centre body line continues around the front, instead of there being a gap as with the plated examples.

Brian Morrison

MK. II HAULAGE

Plate 228 (above): On the bank holiday Monday of 25th May 1981, a relief was needed to the scheduled King's Cross to Leeds express, so No. 31405 was pressed into service to haul the 16.20 'additional' from London. Making an uncommon sight, with air-conditioned stock on a service train, the combination is photographed here passing Hitchin (North) Junction.
Brian Denton

Plate 229 (below): Another really tough job for a Type 2 locomotive. No. 31415 heads a New Year relief to the 13.30 Paddington to Penzance working, on 2nd January 1980, its departure from Paddington being at 13.23. At Iver, Buckinghamshire, where this photograph was taken, the Class 50-hauled 13.30 service was only two minutes behind! The Class 31/4 is fitted for e.t.h., but members of the class are, nevertheless, a rare sight with air-conditioned stock in passenger service.
John Vaughan

A MIDLANDS MIXTURE

Plate 230: British Rail must have been in dire straights, on 14th April 1981, when they could find nothing more powerful than a Type 2 locomotive for the heavy 08.22 Liverpool to Paddington service. Nonetheless, Class 31/4 No. 31424 was only seven minutes behind time when arriving at Leamington Spa for the booked stop.
Brian Morrison

Plate 231: One of the second batch of steam heat-fitted Class 31/1s to be converted to electric train heating was No. 31236, seen here renumbered to 31433 in the sub-classification 31/4, and complete with the new style blue painted roof-mounted marker light panel that identifies them. On 3rd March 1984, the locomotive pulls away from Nuneaton with the 08.04 Birmingham (New Street) to Norwich train.
Brian Morrison

Plate 232: Today, normal passenger services terminate at Walsall, althought at one time, through lines existed for Rugeley, Lichfield and Water Orton. Freight still continues to pass however and, on 2nd March 1984, Stratford-based No. 31112 approaches the station with 'down' ballast hoppers. Electrified local services to Walsall are in the hands of Class 304 and 312 electric multiple units.

Brian Morrison

Plate 233: Sunday engineering work on the ex-Midland Railway line north of Birmingham often results in diversions over the Birmingham to Lichfield route which, otherwise, sees very little but the ubiquitous diesel multiple unit. On 5th October 1980, No. 31200 moves empty coaching stock from Duddeston Carriage Sidings to Leicester, and passes Sutton Coldfield where, at this time, work was advancing for the introduction of colour light signalling. In fact, this signal box closed just two weeks later.

John Whitehouse

CLASS 31 PICTORIAL

Plate 234: Spring blossom at Thetford in Norfolk makes a most attractive frame for No. 31161, pictured leaving the station with the 10.15 Birmingham (New Street) to Norwich service.

John C. Baker

Plate 235: On the sunny evening of 11th September 1978, No. 31222 emerges from Gasworks Tunnel, King's Cross, hauling the 16.20 semi-fast service from Peterborough. At the same time, Class 254 power car No. SC43092, of set No. 254019, prepares to enter with an empty coaching stock working for Bounds Green Depot, where fuelling and servicing will be carried out prior to its next working.

Brian Morrison

Plate 236: About to shatter the peace of a lone passenger, sheltering from the rain inside a platform 'bus shelter' at Maidenhead in Berkshire, on 10th September 1981, is No. 31301, working a parcels service for Old Oak Common.
Geoff Dowling

Plate 237: The branch from Skipton to Grassington & Threshfield was closed to passenger services by the London, Midland & Scottish Railway in 1930, but remains open as far as Rylstone Quarries for transportation of stone to Hull. With a haul of four-wheel Tilcon private owner wagons, No. 31156 meanders along the attractive line in August 1983.
David Wilcock

Plate 238 (right): The setting sun casts a golden hue on to the telegraph wires, rails and flanks of an engineer's train passing Wrabness, on the Harwich branch, on 4th September 1981. Nos. 31112 and 31133 return to Stratford Depot, in East London, having spent the day at Parkeston Quay.
Brian Morrison

MK. III HAULAGE

Plate 239: On Sunday, 1st April 1984, the electric current between Euston and Willesden was cut off, for engineering work to be undertaken in Primrose Hill Tunnel. Electric locomotives and stock had to be diesel-hauled over this stretch, which includes the well-known 1 in 70 gradient of Camden Bank. With a number of Class 25 Bo-Bos being withdrawn, Class 31s are again allocated to Cricklewood, and it was mainly these machines that bore the brunt of the arduous haulage for the day. Empty Mk. III stock, which will form the 12.45 Euston to Glasgow (Central) service glides down the bank behind No. 31289, with Class 85 No. 85006 in tow, and is passed by No. 31283, straining on the upward climb, with Class 86/2 No. 86204 *City of Carlisle* on the 12.00 Euston to Wolverhampton service.

Brian Morrison

Plate 240 (right): On the same day, No. 31213 makes a stirring sight hammering up Camden Bank, with Class 87/0 No. 87034 *William Shakespeare*, and the heavy 11.50 Euston to Manchester (Piccadilly) working in tow.

Brian Morrison